COSMIC WONDER

HALLEY'S COMET and HUMANKIND

Ashley Benham-Yazdani

CANDLEWICK PRESS

The first time the comet visited Earth, nobody noticed.

Well, almost nobody.

C. 200,000 – 16,000 YEARS AGO

The comet had come from far away,
exploring a new path around its star.

It blazed through the cosmos,
let loose its long tail,
and looked down upon the Earth.

C. 200,000 – 16,000 YEARS AGO

In all of its travels, the comet had never seen a planet like this before.

It saw softly shaped clouds that puffed through the sky.

It saw tumbling oceans, deep blue and pale turquoise.

It saw land in all shades of ochre, gray, brown.

And everywhere, it saw life.

C. 200,000 - 16,000 YEARS AGO

Many Earthlings were big, but most were small.
Some held still, with roots reaching deep.
Others moved fast over the ground,
high on the breeze, or underneath waves.

C. 200,000 - 16,000 YEARS AGO

On land many Earthlings walked on four legs.

Some were on two,

but most used even more.

A few had no legs at all, just like the comet.

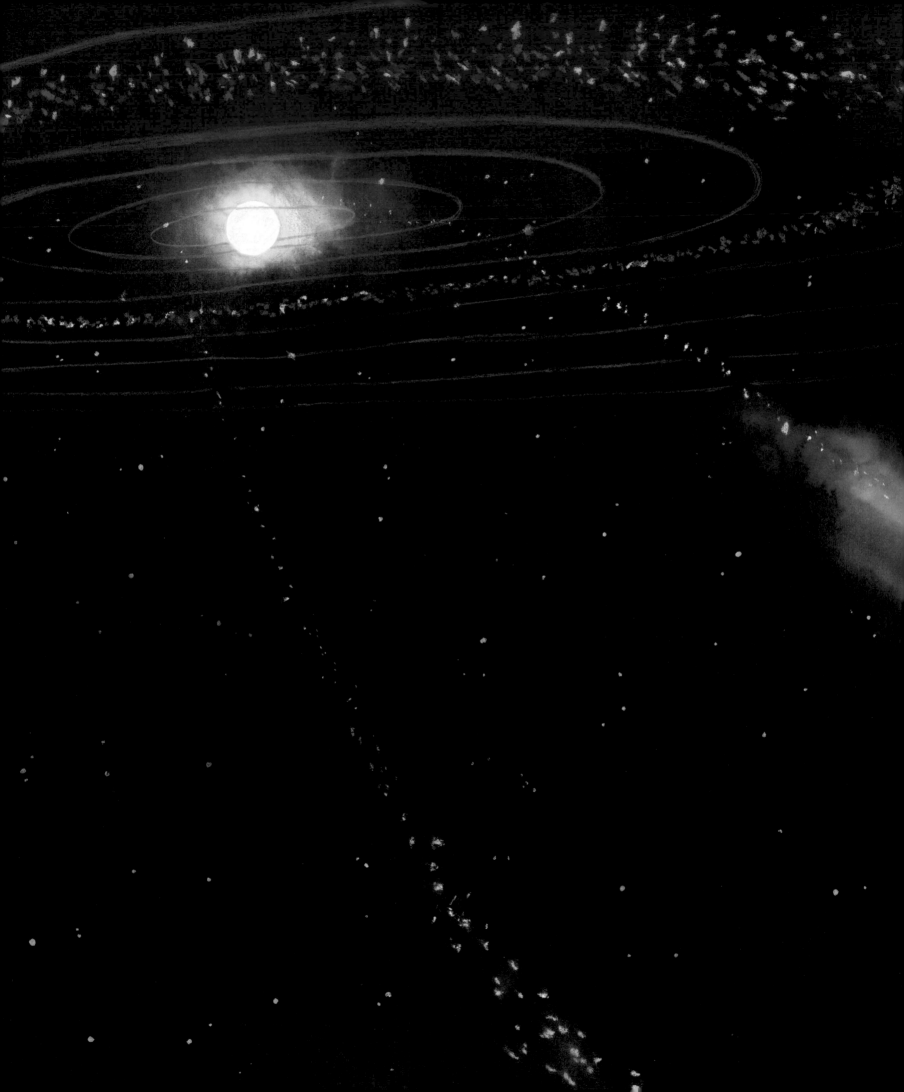

After one quick spin around its star,
the comet sped back past the Earth
and followed its orbit to the darkness of space,
hoping it might return sometime.

And to its delight,
about every seventy-six Earth years,
it did.

The comet visited Earth again and again
for several weeks at a time.
It enjoyed how the Earthlings skittered or soared,
and how others stretched, slow and steady,
grazing the sky with their branches.

The Earthlings moved and ate and lived together,
but after many visits the comet noticed that
one kind of creature began to live differently.

c. 9000 BCE

The humans were changing.

And then they changed again . . .

and again and again.

C. 8000 BCE

c. 7000 BCE

c. 4000 BCE

Now when the comet looked down to the Earth,
the humans gazed right back.
They told each other stories of the "broom star" above,
recording its visits in ink, clay, and words.

466 BCE

240 BCE

164 BCE

141 CE

Between every visit humans changed quickly now,
transforming the Earth with each new discovery.
But at night they still turned their eyes to the sky,
searching the stars for meaning.

The comet thought they were wondrous.
Each one a perfect harmony
of curiosity and creativity.
It wished it could greet each one up close,
but it did not want to frighten them.

And so the comet watched from afar.

1222

The comet saw war.

And it saw peace.

1301

It saw family trees grow tall and wide,
and it saw great minds come and go.

It saw sorrow and joy, wonder and love,
and sometimes many of these feelings
all at once.

1607

What complicated creatures these were!
They were often so cruel to the other Earthlings,
and even to each other.
Sometimes the comet dreaded to visit,
afraid of what it would see.

But it treasured each glimpse
of the humans' greatest power:
boundless love.

1682

1682

1682

After hundreds of visits, the comet arrived
and the humans greeted it with a name:
Halley's Comet.

In all of the comet's ancient life,
it had never had a name before.

1758

Visit after visit, the comet returned.

It saw 1835 and then 1910, when the Earth tickled through its tail.

At the following visit, the comet arrived and found the Earth electrified,

buzzing and hazy on all sides.

Somehow even its shadow side shined.

The comet could see that a lot had happened in just the last seventy-six years.

   It saw billions more humans than ever before.

      It saw that other Earthlings it had known for centuries were now somehow gone.

         It even saw a hole in the sky.

The humans didn't look to the stars much anymore,

and many had forgotten their skittering, soaring, or slow Earthling kin.

But they were still curious.

1986

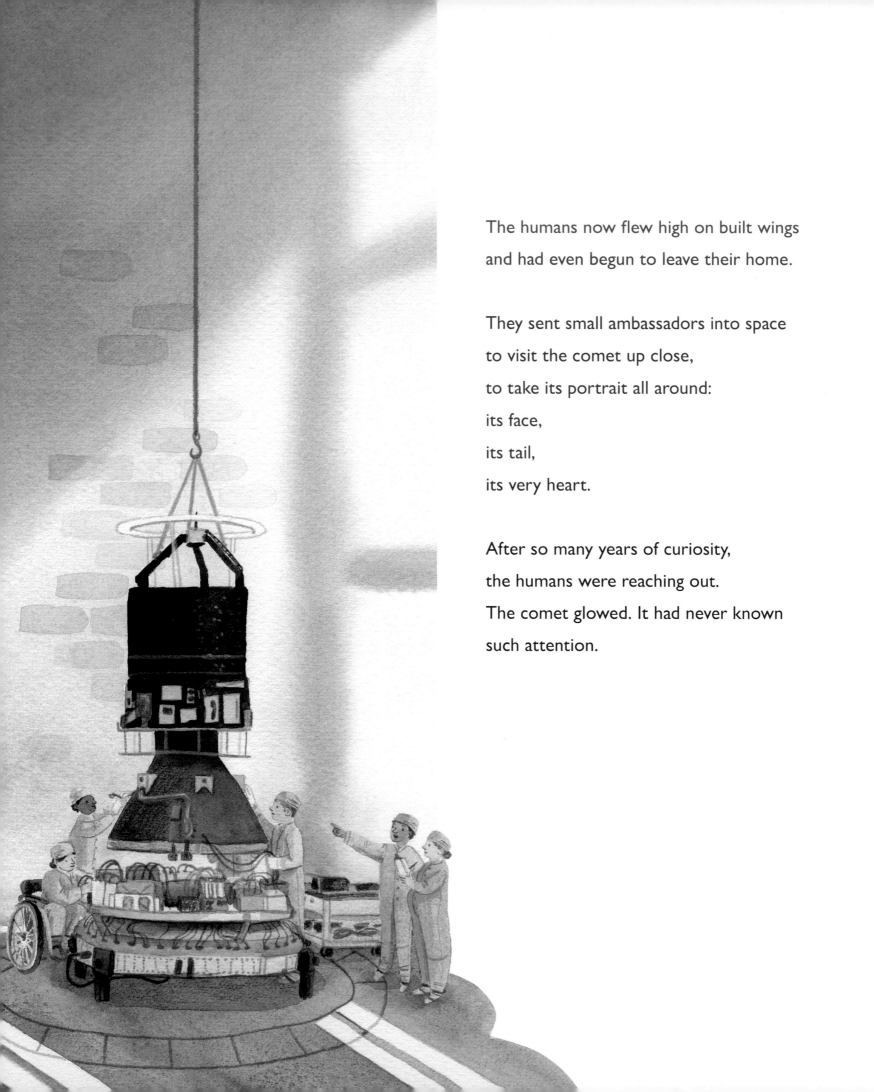

The humans now flew high on built wings
and had even begun to leave their home.

They sent small ambassadors into space
to visit the comet up close,
to take its portrait all around:
its face,
its tail,
its very heart.

After so many years of curiosity,
the humans were reaching out.
The comet glowed. It had never known
such attention.

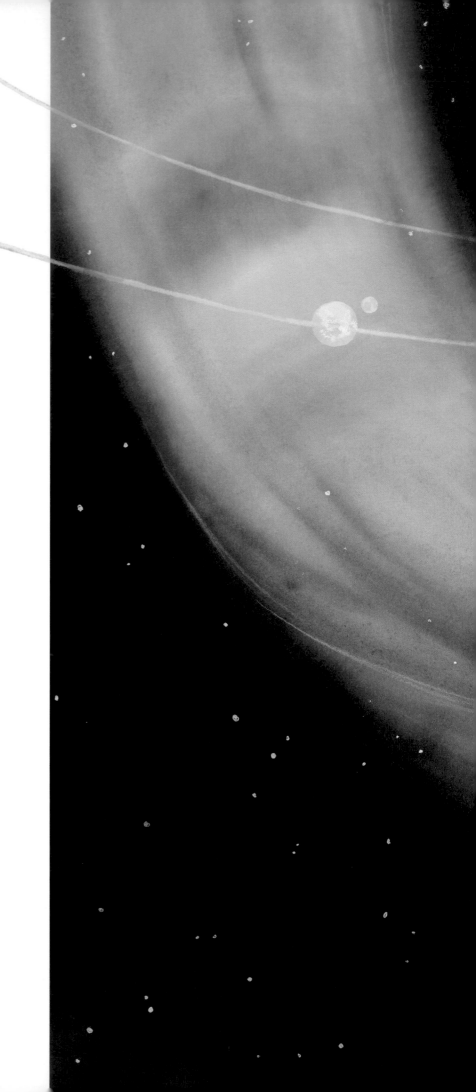

The comet soared again around its star
and looked back once more on the Earth,
the little blue planet it had watched
for thousands and thousands of years.

It was small and vast all at once,
holding so much life and such great promise,
and even more mysteries, still unknown.
Now change was coming faster than ever,
at the hands of the humans below.

The comet flew back out into space,
dreaming of all that had come before
and all it might see the next time.

That was the last time the comet visited Earth,
but it should return in 2061.

2061

When it next dances through the night sky,

it will see an Earth humans don't yet know.

It will see the world they are shaping now.

It might even see you, dear Earthling,

and the future you help to create.

The Comet Observes Earth

EARLY HUMANS

Homo sapiens are known to have existed 300,000 years ago. At first we were not the only human creatures on our planet, and we coexisted with others similar to us, including Neanderthals and Denisovans. Neanderthals died out about 40,000 years ago but still live on in one way: each of us carries a tiny bit of Neanderthal DNA, and many people also carry Denisovan DNA.

THE CUEVA DE LAS MANOS

This early example of human artwork in present-day Argentina dates from 9,000 to 13,000 years ago and features colorful stencils of hundreds of hands, as well as painted abstract symbols and images of animals. Most of the hand silhouettes are left hands, and the artists likely made them by blowing pigment through a pipe.

THE FIRST BIG CHANGE

Humans began growing food for themselves about 9,000 years ago, during the Neolithic Revolution. With this development of agriculture, humans began settling down and cities were born. The early cities pictured in this book are Çatalhöyük, in present-day Turkey, and Nabta Playa, in present-day southern Egypt, home to the earliest known astronomers, who built a large stone circle that aligned with the stars.

THE BROOM STAR

Chinese astronomers made the earliest known records of Halley's Comet in 240 BCE, describing it as a "broom star." Since then, Halley's Comet has been depicted many times, including in Babylonian texts in 164 BCE and in the Bayeux Tapestry, a 230-foot (70-meter) embroidered work from the eleventh century that chronicles the 1066 Norman invasion of England.

WAR AND PEACE

Genghis Khan would have seen Halley's Comet in 1222. It is thought that he took the comet's westward-seeming trajectory as a sign that he should also move west, conquering as he went. Also shown are the Hopi, a Native American tribe whose full name, Hopituh Shi-nu-mu, translates to "The Peaceful People." This name reflects a peace that lasted for centuries, broken only when the Hopi were directly threatened by European colonists in the late seventeenth century.

HUMAN EXPANSION

Halley's Comet would have seen humans explore the entire Earth. Some of these travelers were the Polynesian way finders, who sailed the Pacific in sturdy voyaging canoes, navigating by the sun, stars, and ocean currents.

CELESTIAL INSPIRATION

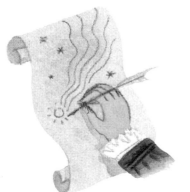

William Shakespeare was one of many great thinkers to witness a comet. During his lifetime, he saw several comets, including Halley's visit in 1607. He even referenced these mysterious visitors in some of his plays:

*"By being seldom seen, I could not stir
But like a comet I was wondered at."*
(*Henry IV,* Part 1, Act 3)

WHAT WAS THAT HOLE IN THE SKY?

In 1986 Halley's Comet may have noticed some depletion of the ozone layer. This "hole" was caused by human-made chemicals that were breaking down ozone, letting more solar radiation through the atmosphere. These chemicals have since been banned, and the hole is healing.

Earth Observes the Comet

THE COMET'S ORIGINS

Halley's Comet likely formed around the same time as
the rest of our solar system about 4.6 billion years ago. It
drifted far from Earth until between 200,000 and 16,000
years ago, when it began its present orbit around the sun.
This orbit is long and narrow, taking an average of
seventy-six Earth years to complete. The point in a comet's
orbit when it is closest to the sun is called perihelion. The
point farthest from the sun is called aphelion.

WHAT IS A COMET?

Comets are chunks of ice, frozen gas, and dust—this solid
mass is called the nucleus. When they approach a star,
some of the ice evaporates, creating a bright aura, called
a coma, and a vapor tail. The nucleus also sheds debris,
leaving a second tail of solid matter in the comet's
wake. Sometimes a comet's two tails point in different
directions, but the vapor tail always points away from the
sun. Because comets lose ice and debris every time they
pass a star, they have a finite life span. Some last
for many orbits; others last for only one.

METEOR SHOWERS

The dust and debris shed by comets stay in space. When
Earth passes through a comet's orbit, it can encounter
this debris, which falls in a meteor shower. The orbit of
Halley's Comet causes two annual meteor showers: the Eta
Aquarid in May and the Orionid in October.

WHO WAS HALLEY?

Edmond Halley (rhymes with "valley") was an English
astronomer and mathematician who theorized that
comets from 1531, 1607, and 1682 were one repeat
visitor, which he calculated would return in 1758. It did,
but Halley did not live to see his theory proven. In
honor of his discovery, the comet was given his name.
Astronomers now call it 1P/Halley, 1P meaning the first
periodic (predictably returning) comet discovered.

SPACE EXPLORATION

Before the comet's 1986 visit, astronomers around the
world worked to create the Halley Armada: a series of
probes that were sent to collect data. The first Armada
probes were Vega 1 and 2 (from Soviet Russia) and
Suisei and Sakigake (from Japan). Data from these probes
made it possible for Giotto, from the European Space
Agency, to bring its camera closest of all—within 372
miles (600 kilometers) of Halley's nucleus.

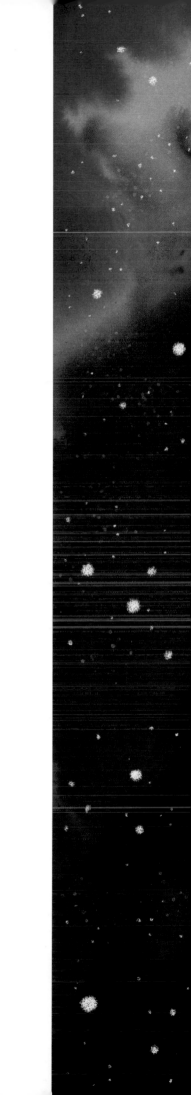

Author's Note

Looking back on the entirety of known human history could make one feel distant from the past, but in producing this book I was surprised to feel closer to it than ever. The research reframed my sense of time, telescoping it until the distant past felt more present. I came to see time as a fine thread that connects us all. It ties us to every inventor, explorer, and dreamer who came before, leading us all the way back to our earliest common ancestor. These realizations were all the more poignant to me working out this book idea as a new parent, glimpsing the past, present, and future all at once in my own tiny baby.

Our long-term comet visitor has seen many of the discoveries, wonders, and, sadly, numerous tragedies of humanity, including our devastating impact on the planet. In all of its visits, one thing has been unchanging: the human hope that our children's lives will be better, safer, happier than our own. We have had some strange ways of trying to ensure this in the past, but we can do better now, and the stakes are higher than ever as a disaster of our own making—the climate crisis—threatens to sever the thread of humanity's time. It will take great work to mitigate this existential threat, but I still have hope that we will make the effort to ensure that humanity's future is bright, not brief. We owe it to our ancestors who strove to bring us here, to our animal and plant kin that we share this planet with, and to our children, who are now standing alongside us in this work.

The thread of time that unites us leads in both directions: it goes back to the past, but it also runs through our actions, tying us to the future. Thanks to those who came before, we are well equipped to improve this future. We each possess the same ingenuity of the best of our ancestors, as well as the gift of knowledge they gave us. We have all the benefits of modern science, and for the first time in history we have global connection at our fingertips. All that remains is to uncover the collective will to change, the desire to cooperate, and the drive to persist. My fellow human, we have all that, too. It's been there since the beginning. Now, in the present moment, we each have a part to play in weaving the thread of our future, and we each have a little time. Just imagine what you can accomplish with all of that.

Bibliography

Asimov, Isaac. *Asimov's Guide to Halley's Comet*. New York: Nightfall, 1985.

Etter, Roberta, and Stuart Schneider. *Halley's Comet: Memories of 1910*. New York: Abbeville Press, 1985.

Harari, Yuval Noa. *Sapiens: A Brief History of Humankind*. New York: Harper Perennial, 2015.

Sagan, Carl. "You Are Here." Chap. 1 in *Pale Blue Dot*. New York: Random House, 1994.

*For my children—Rowan, who brought me this story
in our earliest days together, and Willow, who arrived just
before its completion—with boundless love*

First edition 2023

Library of Congress Catalog Card Number 2022922784
ISBN 978-1-5362-2323-1

23 24 25 26 27 28 LEO 10 9 8 7 6 5 4 3 2 1

Printed in Heshan, Guangdong, China

This book was typeset in Gill Sans MT Pro.
The illustrations were done in mixed media.

Candlewick Press
99 Dover Street
Somerville, Massachusetts 02144

www.candlewick.com